# Retire A Millionaire!

*How to safely invest and manage your money for your retirement planning and retire wealthy.*

By Sean Dematrés

## Introduction

Hello, my name is Sean Dematrés.
I am an entrepreneur and investor from Germany. And before you ask me about my last name, yes I do have french roots.

I have never had much to do with books business wise, except reading a lot of them of course. But the reason I decided to start writing is that I believe that I have a very important message to share.

Every morning I see troubled and sad faces around me. And its because these people are trapped in our financial system, they run in circles, and most of us do. They earn money to pay bills and once they get promoted and earn more money they usually have to pay more bills.
There is this constant fear that we wont have enough money by the end of the month.
There is this constant fear that if your boss lets you go, you will be homeless in less than a month or two.
In my mind nobody should have so much power over my life. This is scary.

These people are trapped in the system and therefore they are being robbed of their freedom.
And most of them don't even notice, for them that is just the way it is: earn money, pay bills.

I would be miserable as well if I was in this position, working in a more or less dead end job and being at the might of other people.

But I was lucky enough to learn how to play the game of money.

To break out of this system you will have to understand how it works and how you can use it to your advantage.
And that is what I am trying to teach in this book.

It probably wont be easy, you will have to work a little harder and be a little smarter but don't worry, everybody who truly wants to be financial independent can be. Those who don't achieve it are just not willing to make any sacrifice at all.

What would you give when your boss tries to enforce another silly company policy and you are able to say: "STOP! I don't need to put up with this. I don't need your money and I am the one who decides with whom I make business with."

Telling my boss that I can decide who I make business with in front of all my coworkers was one of the best feelings in my life.
But you have to get you money right to be able to do that. You don't need enormous amounts of money, you just have to invest it intelligently and don't waste it.

I wish for you and everybody who reads my books that you will come into the enjoyment of becoming financially free and being able to decide how and with whom you spend your time.

Because your time is the most valuable currency we have, spend it wisely.

Thank you

# Table of Contents:

# The Golden Rule

When you are young, at times retirement seems so far off that you do not think you have to prepare any time soon. However, retirement is a plan that you need to put in action now rather than later. If you want to retire with a lot of money, then you need to start now.

This book has a lot to offer you when it comes to strategising your retirement. If you would like to retire a millionaire, then you will need to dive in now. It takes time and patience to build up the retirement fund. Investments are the main way to get your retirement funds right where they need to be and where you want them to be.

Investing in real estate will take a couple years to begin in the right manner. This means that you have to start now to get you where you want to be. With determination you can get to become a millionaire and do whatever it is that you would like to do in your golden years. Read through your options and how to get started.

There is one golden rule if you want to become a wealthy person. It is so easy but most people have never heard of it or simply don't follow it.

<u>Invest in assets and avoid liabilities!</u>

It doesn't get simpler than this. You just have to invest in things that put money in your pocket like real estate, businesses or collectors items and avoid things that take money out of your pocket like a new car or consumer debt.

This book gives you an overview and basic understanding on which are the most common investments that make money and how they work.
Please only invest after you informed yourself throughly about your investment and the market.

With that said let's jump right into it.

# Chapter 1: Importance of Retirement Funds

Having a retirement plan set into place is detrimental for your survival once you get older. Within this book you are going to learn different ways to ensure that you retire with a healthy and full bank account; however, first in this chapter we are covering why you need to make sure you feed the bank account.

## Uncertainty of Pension Benefits and Social Security

First off, you need to understand the prospects of the government sponsored retirement plans are not good. The developed world populations are ageing continuously, with lesser working aged people to keep in the workforce to contribute to the social security plan systems. For example, consider that in 2005 a study was conducted by Stephen Goss, which is the chief actuary of the Social Security Administration. The ratio that covered workers versus the amount of beneficiaries under the United States Social Security program has reduced greatly over the years. In the year 1940, there were 35 million workers that were paying into the social security system with only 222,000 retired beneficiaries. The ratio is 159 to 1. In the year 2003, the number of the workers then increased to 154 million, and there were approximately 47 million beneficiaries. The ratio then was 3.3 to 1.

The pattern is very similar to exist with the pension systems as well. This includes those that are located in the European nations. Simultaneously the burdens that are put on the system keeps getting greater and greater. This is due to more people retiring and it is also due to the advances in health care. People are living longer, which means that there is more money being paid out that there was in the past years.

This double effect holds the potential to put a large strain on the system and it can leave the governments with no viable option but to lower the social security benefits or to suspend them completely except for the ones that are extremely poor.

Private pension plans are not immune to the shortcomings. Corporate collapses, like the high profile bankruptcy of the company Enron can result in the employer to be wiped out along with the pension plan.

Defined benefit pension plans, which is supposed to be able to guarantee the participants a specific monthly pension for a specified amount of time through their retirement years can fail. It at times requires an increase of contributions from the sponsors of the plan, benefits reductions, or at times, both. This is to keep the plan operating.

In addition, there are many employers who used to offer their employees defined benefit plans, but now are shifting to defined contribution plans due to the increase of the liability and the expenses that are associated with the defined benefit plans. This means that it increases the uncertainty of the security of the retirement for many people. The uncertainties have been transferred to the financing of retirement from the employers and the government to the individuals, this then leaves them with no choice.

## Unanticipated Medical Expenses

While the failure of social security may not happen, planning for your own retirement on funds that you do not control is not the greatest of options. Even if you put the risk of that aside, it is important to understand that social security will not provide you with an adequate retirement fund. By definition, the social security programs are meant to offer a basic safety net, which is the bare minimum of the standard of living.

Without additional savings to add to the safety net, you will find it very difficult or impossible to enjoy much of the minimum standard of living that the social security provides. This situation is able to quickly become very alarming if your health deteriorates.

Old age does typically bring on different medical issues and increased health expenses. Without your own additional nest egg, living in your golden years will be hard while trying to take care of the burden of health expenses. In order to prevent an unforeseen illness from taking up your savings, you will need to consider getting insurance like medical, as well as long term care insurance, also called LTC in order to finance the health care needs as they arise.

## Estate Planning

Switching to a positive angle, consider your family and your loved ones for just a moment. Part of the retirement savings will help contribute to your kids and your grandchildren, be it for education, passing it on, or keeping sentimental assets like real estate or land inside the family.

Without a planned out retirement nest egg, you will be forced to liquidate the assets in order to pay the expenses during the retirement years. This can prevent you from leaving a legacy for the loved ones, or even worse, it can cause you to become a burden on your family financially in your older age.

## Flexibility to Deal with Different Changes

Life tends to throw curve balls here and there. Unforeseen illnesses, financial needs of dependents, and the uncertainty of the social security plan are only a few that can play a key factor in a devastating retirement plan. Regardless of these challenges faced in life, a nest egg that is secure will give a lot of help when it comes time to help. Financial hiccups are smoothed over when a secure plan is set in place.

# Chapter 2: Real Estate

With the typical plans for retirement being depleted, there are other ways that you can make money to put towards your plan. In this chapter we are going to dive into different options that you are able to utilize to ensure your future with real estate. In this chapter you are going to learn about different property types that one could use in order to make money. Here is a list of different properties and what they mean for your future.

- **Raw Land**: This is about as raw as it gets. Purchasing land that does not produce any cash flow can give you the potential for value. Land can be purchased cheap and then divided in order to sell off pieces for a larger profit. You can even develop the land in order to build a cashflow system like a hotel, duplex, mall, and more.

- **Farm Investing**: Not only does the land offer a way to build cash, but you can also offer a way of selling different products in order to make a good profit. Most farms produce more than one product. For example, a farm may produce corn, as well as wheat or even eggs from chickens. The land can be developed in order to offer more than one way of building your bank account.

- **Mineral, Water, Gas, Oil Rights**: This is the cousin of investing in the raw land, this is the process of which you buy and sell a company's (or person's) right to use the water, minerals, gas, oil, etc on a piece of property.

- **Single Family Residences**: This is one of the main investments for most people, especially first time investors. These homes are very easy to rent out, easy to sell on the market, and easy to finance. These can be harder for a cash flow, and it can take a big amount of time, as well as effort, but you can build on this. We will go over this in another section since this is one of the easiest ways to build your bank account up for retirement.

- **Duplex, Triplex, and Quads**: These are small multifamily properties that normally consist of two to four units. This is one of many investments that prove to be a favourite way to invest in real estate and make money. This type of property combine the financing and is easy to purchase. They offer more benefits than a single family home. They offer more cash flow and has less competition. They also serve as a solid investment, as well as a residence on a personal level for the smartest of investors. This will also be covered in more detail.

- **Small Apartments**: Another favourite of investors is small apartment buildings. They are made up of anywhere from five up to fifty units per building. This type of property can at times be more difficult to finance as they rely on commercial lending standards and not residential lending. However, these types of properties are great in the terms of cash flow. They are too small for the professional REITs to invest in; however, they are too large for the novice of investors. Additionally, the value of this type of property are based on the income that they bring in. This creates a very large opportunity for adding in value by increasing the unit rent, decreasing the expenses, as well as managing effectively. This type of properties are a great place to use an on site manager who will manage and perform different maintenance in exchange for decreased rent. At this level, the real estate will truly become at least 90 percent passive income.

- **Large Apartment Buildings**: This type of building is larger, much nicer complexes that you see all around, and often times is in the upper-middle class type neighbourhoods located in the suburbs. They are often times offering amenities like pools, full time staff, work out rooms, and high advertising budgets. This type of properties cost tens of millions in order to buy, but will produce a huge and solid return with a small amount of hassle.

- **Small Commercial Office Space**: Purchasing a small commercial building and renting out the space to business professionals will offer a good cash flow. Often times these are more hands on.

- **Large Commercial Office Space**: Purchasing large commercial buildings and renting out the space to business professionals is a good way for cash flow. Typically a professional will manage a large property of this type.

- **Industrial Properties**: This type of property includes business types like warehouses, manufacturing warehouses, distribution centres, and more.

- **Mobile Homes**: Typically these are found in parks, but they are also on private land. Mobile homes are all over the country, and they can be an inexpensive way in order to enter the real estate world. They can also provide an significant way to get cash flow.

- **Mobile Home Parks**: The mobile home park is a park in which mobile homes are placed on it and can be purchased and sold. Often times the lots are rented out to the owners of the mobile home and other times the homes are corporately owned and then leased to the individuals. This is a good cash flow system and we will go into how to start this for your retirement.

- **Notes**: When a person invests in notes it involves purchasing and selling of paper mortgages. While this is not necessarily a type of property, notes can be purchased, sold, mortgaged, and can be traded just like the properties that they represent. Often times an owner of this property can choose to offer financing and they can carry the mortgage. In that case, a note can be created which then spells out the terms of a contract. For example, and apartment owner that decides to sell the property for one million dollars. He can also offer to carry the full note and the newer buyer will then make payments of eight percent of the year for at least thirty years, until the full amount is paid off. If the owner suddenly needs to get the full balance of the specified loan, they may choose to sell the mortgage to a note buyer for a specified discount. That same note buyer will begin to collect the payments and decide if they want to keep the note or sell it for a good amount of profit.

- **International Real Estate Investing**: You do not need to actually live where you are investing, although it does help. Many different investors decide to live where they invest, but other investors invest where it makes most sense. This includes overseas. While there are many different challenges to this type, there are also large rewards to those who decide to go across international waters.

- **Lease Option**: A lease option is a method that is utilised to control real estate without taking the title. Is it simply just renting the property with a right to purchase it later. This is able to offer a good way to purchase a property if the intent is to sell it fast at a later date.

- **For Sale by Owner**: This is also called FSBO. This is where you purchase a home and you list it for sale yourself. This will cut out the middle man, also known as the real estate agent, which you will pay. This will keep the money in the bank account instead of a middle man's hand.

- **Pre-Foreclosure Purchase**: There are sellers that are on the brink of just losing their home to the bank and are extremely motivated to sell the home and to save their credit. Often times, more is owed on the home than the house is actually worth. However, at times there are many great deals that can be found by just weeding out the bad deals.

- **HUD Foreclosures**: Then the United States government insured home is foreclosed on, often times it will become the property of the department of Housing and Urban Development. It is then their job to sell the house and it will offer a steeper discount in order to move the home. These can be extremely good deals for those who would like to flip homes.

# Single Home Residences: Fix and Flip Homes

Flipping homes is a great way to get that money in the bank for your future. It is essentially purchasing a house or property with an intent to sell it later for a good profit. However, the logistics can get complicated. There are many decisions that go into beginning through the flipping process.One question and decision that kick starts the process is to decide where you will purchase your first home to flip. If you buy a house in an neighbourhood that is up and coming, you are banking on the neighbourhood to increase in its value.

If you decide to purchase a new development, then you will want to attract higher end type home buyers that want luxury features and a lot of space. If things go well, then you can make a very large profit. However, if something does not go as planned like timing issues, faulty budgeting, or a crime spikes, then you will be stuck with this house that you are unable to sell.

Once you know where to purchase the home, the next step is to decide what property type you would like to purchase. If you decide on a fixer-upper, then you are committing to improving this home. This will take time, as well as money. If you purchase a property that is foreclosed on during an auction or from a certain bank, then you can get a bargain on a underpriced house. However, remember that if the previous homeowner could not pay the mortgage, then they probably could not pay for the property upkeep. You may have to deal with an infestation or even a leaky roof. There is no telling what you may be getting into.

Those homes that are deemed fixer-uppers or foreclosures are what most investors think of when they want to flip homes. However, it is quite possible to flip a home without doing any maintenance at all. During the real estate boom in the mid-2000s, flippers were able to purchase new construction homes, were able to hold on to them for a couple months, then they could sell them for a good profit. How there is a trend toward flipping houses in a new, high end type of development in outlying suburbs. If retail and commercial development spring up, it can bring in droves of the residents. However, if the situation is not perfect, like gas prices go up, it can cause a homebuyer to shy away from these commutes. This type of flipping can be risky.

If you watch the home and garden channels, it may appear as if everyone is flipping home. There are many people have created careers out of purchasing distressed homes and turning them around quickly for a good profit. However, in real estate things are not so easy as the television shows suggest.

The very first piece of advice that flipping experts offer is to make a good budget and stick to it. While you find a perfect place and you know that your skill set is important, budgeting is where flippers will often times make their mistake. So where should you begin? First, you will need to get financing. This step is typically pretty easy. This type of mortgage will allow purchasers to pay little to no down payment. In exchange, they are responsible for higher interest rates. However, when you are planning on purchasing a house and only keeping it for a few months, that is a very small issue. When the market seems to be flat, obtaining a mortgage for a property for investment can be difficult. A high interest rate will empty the investor's wallet if the property sits.

What this means is that cash plays a big role in getting the house to flip. The larger down payment that you can put down, the lower the interest rate will be. You will also need cash in order to fix the home in order to flip it. In the next section you will learn how to make a budget for the flip. This budget can also be used on the other types of property. Keep in mind that if an offer sounds like it is too good to be true, it probably is. This also goes for the perfect, underpriced property, as well as for the friendly contractor. You will always need to ask for some references from the contractor.

If you are planning to purchase a new construction home, budgeting can prove to be easy. It is just like purchasing a home that you plan on living in, you will need to cover the insurance, mortgage, real estate agent, taxes, and even lawyer fees. However, in a market that is softening, the supply of homes is greater than the demand, this means that you may own a property longer than you have anticipated. Therefore you must do your research. If you are working on a home that is a fixer upper, then the budget will begin to grow once you consider the renovation that you will need to make. According to the experts, you will need to add twenty percent to the estimate in order to cover the final costs. If you end up overestimating the budget, then you will get a windfall, but if you underestimate the budget, then you are stuck with unexpected expenses.

Structural improvements like electrical, plumbing, insulation, HVAC, and pest control are typically the most important and the most seen improvements that a flipper will need to make. New floors and pain will get buyers inside the doors; however, a termite problem will kill your deal fast. If you do not have the right technical skills, then you will have to figure in the cost of buying labor.

Most real estate agents will advise fixing up a kitchen and bathrooms for a good return on the investment. In addition to this, you may need to purchase new counters, cabinets, hardware, backsplashes, sinks, floors, appliances, and lighting. Kitchen upgrades may prove to be a bit pricey, but they will make a large impression and will ultimately improve your return. You may also decide that you should go green, which will add additional value to the home when the improvements add to the marketing. You will be able to keep your costs down if the home is in good structural repair and just needs some fresh paint and carpets. However, things can get pricey if you are using contractors or outside labor.

Another aspect when considering a home should be curb appeal. The outside of the home is important. You may need to paint the outside, fix up the landscape, or even fix the driveway, which will add to the budget the that you have planned out. However, it will also drive up the value of the property and give you a better return. It will also give you better chances of selling the property. If you have purchased a home in a pricey neighbourhood, mowing the grass and repairing the fence may not even be enough. There may be a homeowner association fee. You will need to find out if there is.

## Make Money with Apartment Buildings

Making money with apartment buildings may take time. You will need to find the right building and that can take some time. You will need to know what you are getting into. You will work pretty hard to find a building that is good and is a fair price. Here is how owning an apartment building works:

Imagine that you close on a building and the property manager ends up taking over. If you ask other apartment owners, they will explain that they only spend about two to five hours a week on their building if they have hired the right management company. With this little time and large return, you can build up your apartment empire. If you have two apartment complexes then you would only spend four to ten hours a week and getting so much money in return. This is less than a part time job. You can spend your golden years doing whatever it is that you want with a tremendous amount of money. Let us go into how to make money on your investments.

The value of a building is driven up by net operating income. This is the amount of income that is left after the expenses are paid. The more money that the building spits out after the expenses, the more it is worth.

In many different parts of the country, a building is worth ten times the net operating income. This is called a 10 times multiplier. It is referred to as capitalisation or a cap rate. Do not worry about this. It is not important to the point. Let us use a cap rate of ten for this example.

Let us use the example of a building with the net operating income $100,000. This would make it worth one million dollars. If you are able to make the building generate at least $10,000 more every year, then by increasing the rent or decreasing the expenses, you will generate $100,000 in value.

Assume that you purchased a 20 unit building for the price of $540,000 and then you put 30 percent down. The building was bought at a 10 cap rate based on the formula. This means the net operating income is $54,000 each year, times the cap rate of ten is $540,000. The income per unit should be $1,000 and the expenses are fifty-five percent of the income. The building is in good shape and is being managed by the owner. So far there isn't anything special about the deal.

However, suppose that you have found out that the average market rent in this specific area is $200 higher monthly, and suppose that you meet a property manager who manage two other buildings that are similar in the area and they tell you that the expenses are 45 percent of the income. Now, the units are bringing in $1,200 monthly and the lowered expenses are only 45 percent of the income. Here is how this would impact the financials. By doing these two things you have added $25,000 to the net operating income. Now, the value is $790,000. There is an increase of $250,000.
The numbers go like this:

The down payment was $160,000 and the total profit if you should sell the building in three years is $284,000. This actually means that you doubled the investment. However, in the meantime you have enjoyed the average of $3,500 monthly cash flow. However, in the name of what you are trying to do you should keep it. $3,500 is not enough to live on and become a rich retired person. What this means is that you should purchase another building, and then another. If you become a small apartment building empire then you can rest assured that by retirement you will have the money you want by time you are ready to retire.

# Vacation Rentals

Vacation rentals are a bit like flipping, but you are not going to sell the home once you have it fixed up. With the housing market down, it is a good time to jump into this type of real estate in order to build your retirement funds. Investing in this real estate can be very profitable. Not only is the current housing prices low, but if you are able to turn it into a rental property, then you can end up making a very large monthly profit. It will depend on how much you rent it out for. In order to get the best deals, check with the banks for foreclosing lists. Just be careful of the property's condition.

Since it can be riskier to invest in real estate with an idea of flipping it for a profit, keeping the property on a long term basis as a rental property is ideal. When the market goes up then you can decide if you would like to hold it as a rental or not.

**Offsetting the Expenses**
- Deduce the mortgage interest expense, you will need to use the home for fourteen days out of a year or ten percent of the total days that you rent out the vacation home, whichever one is longer in order for it to qualify as a second home. This is an expense that is deducted no matter the amount of rent that you bring in. It is a second home expense.
- Obviously there will be income to claim from rentals. You are able to deduct the expenses that are related to the property at a percentage of the home. So, if the house is rented 85 days in a year and you will use it at least 15 days, the percentage would be 85/99 or 86 percent. You will deduct the the expenses from the net profit.

**Do Your Homework**
Before you purchase a cottage or a cabin it is important to do your research. First of all, you need to qualify for a loan. There is no sense in getting involved if you do not qualify. Most banks or other financial institution have applications online. This will make it easy to find out where you are able to get the best mortgage and rate.

Other things to consider include utilities. How much will it cost to provide heat, water, electricity, etc. You will need to ensure that the vacationing family pays for their use of utilities so that it does not cut into your profit. Look at the surrounding rental properties and see what the cost would be to rent it out per week. You can increase the cost since this is a temporary rent and not a permanent rental. Another thing to remember is that you may need to repair the property. Make sure to charge a maintenance fee or a security deposit in order to cover any costs of repairing the property.

# Chapter 3: Safe Investment Options

In this chapter you are going to learn about investment portfolios and safe investment options in order to build your bank account up for your retirement years. One of the trickiest thing about beginning investing is to understand the jargon and the lingo that everyone else uses. There are many different terms that are thrown into the mix which can make it difficult to understand. One of the commonly misunderstood terms that are used is investment portfolio. But what is it exactly?

An investment portfolio is a mix of investment types that are held simultaneously, and it is a method of decreasing or even limiting the risk that is associated with the process of investing. By balancing a portfolio you will limit the risk of being left to the side during an investment option or earnings.

**Portfolio Items**

A portfolio is able to encompass any combination of investment types , including bonds, bank accounts, stocks, deeds, warrants, futures, businesses, and certificates. Any item that can retain the value or produce a return is able to be included in the investment portfolio.

The types of items that are included in the portfolio are based on individual circumstances and the investment goals. The very first thing that you will want to do is decide what your investment budget is and what goal you ultimately want to achieve through the action of investing.

Different types of investment vehicles offer different return rates. Each vehicle will carry its own unique amount of risk. Understand the investments that are available to you and how each can be utilized to reach the financial goals you have set into place. It is essential to know what to include in the investment portfolio.

**Establishing the Investment Portfolio**

A financial adviser will help you make smart decisions in regards to what investments that you need in the portfolio. He or she will also be able to aid you in figuring out how many of each investments that you should include. Establishing an investment portfolio can take some time and getting it balanced in the right way can take a bit longer especially for those that have limited capital for investments.

You may have an investment portfolio now and not even know that you do. Let us say for example that you have a few small investments that are located in different areas. Perhaps you have an interest in savings accounts with the local bank, one bond that was given to you during Christmas when you were a kid, and a few stocks that you bought on a whim. All of these in combination make up an investment portfolio. Granted, it is not an impressive of balanced one, but it is still a portfolio.

### Balancing the Portfolio

An investment portfolio should be built in a way that you can achieve financial goals. Having a small handful of investment, but no large investment is not going to get you anywhere in retirement or even pay for a child's college education. In order to get where you want to be you will need to put some work into the portfolio. Figure out what you would like to achieve and then you will build your portfolio in order to meet the goals. There are different kinds of investments that carry a varying degree of risk and then offer different return of rates. Balancing the portfolio to manage the risk and still getting the greatest return is possible if there is a goal.

### Sub Portfolios and Asset Bundles

The investment portfolio might contain a number of sub portfolios or even investment bundles. For example, a stock portfolio is diversified sub portfolio that has stocks in different sectors and industries that limit the risk of losing stock investments.

Shares that are included in the portfolio are able to be diversified by selecting stocks from different sized businesses and companies, as well as different structures. You can also have a large cap, publicly traded stocks to small caps, shares are held in a cooperative.

Some investors refer to the sub portfolios are deemed asset bundles. These bundles are able to be compared to the other portfolio options in order to determine the overall investment portfolio. In such analysis, assets are then slotted into bundles according to the similarities and the performance of each of the bundles.

**Well Balanced Portfolio Through Industry Analysis and Stock Sectors**

A general comparison in the way stocks in sector perform can be a benefit to the investor in choosing different stocks for inclusion in a balanced portfolio. Spreading the stock holdings over many sectors allow an investor to minimise their risk.

By spreading the stock holdings over different sectors you will lessen the chances of losing all of the investments should a crisis come into play. For example, a crisis which hits the sector financially there will be residual impact on other sectors within the market. However, it will have a limited impact on the overall stock holdings provided that you do not have every investment in just one sector.

# 9 Safe and Sound Investment Options

In this section you will be able to learn about the top nine safest investments to save for you retirement fund. It will make your golden years great. Each of the investments on this list is safe and a great way to get your portfolio going and save for a large retirement fund.

1. **Construct a Return Portfolio**: One of the most common ways to create a good retirement income is to build your own portfolio of bonds and stocks, or you can work with a good financial advisor. The portfolio is created to achieve a respectable long term return, and along the way you are able to follow a set of withdrawal rate rules. That will allow you to take about approximately four to seven percent a year. You will be able to withdraw more in years to come. The concept behind the return is that you are targeting a 10 to 20 year average yearly return that will meet or even exceed the withdrawal rate. Although you may be targeting a long term type average, in any year the return will deviate from the average a bit. In order to follow this type of investment you will have to maintain a diversified allocation even if there are year to year ups and downs in the portfolio.

2. **Retirement Income Funds**: Retirement income funds are a type of mutual fund. They are automatically allocate the money across a portfolio that is diversified of bands and stocks. Often times it is by owning a selection of different mutual funds. The investments are then managed with a goal in mind of producing a monthly incomes that is given to you. These funds are constructed in order to provide a package that will accomplish a certain objective. Some of the funds may have an objective of producing a

higher income monthly and may use some of the principal to meet the payout objectives. Other funds may have a lower monthly income target which in combination of the goal will preserve the principal. With a retirement fund you will then retain control of the principal and is able to access the money whenever it is that you want.

3. **Immediate Annuities**: All annuities are a form of insurance rather than a type of investment. These are included on the list due to the purpose of having them. They are used to produce an income and that is what is needed for retirement. With an immediate annuity, you are providing insurance to your future income. In exchange for a payment, the insurance company will provide you with a guarantee of income for life. The guarantee is as strong as a regular insurance company. There are fixed immediate and variable immediate annuities. Some will offer an income that will increase with the rate of inflation, although that actually means that you will start out receiving a lower income monthly. You can choose the term of the annuity like a ten year payout or a joint life payout. You can even choose a single life payout. Immediate annuities are also able to be a good solution for those people who do not have other sources of income that is guaranteed.

4. **Buy Bonds**: Once you purchase a bond you will loan the money to either a corporation, the government, or a municipality. The borrower will agree to pay you some interest for a specified amount of time and when the bond matures, you will get the principal back. The interest income you receive from the bond can be a source of retirement income that is steady. Bonds that have quality rating will give you an idea of the strength it has. There are short, mid, and long term bonds. There are also different bonds that have adjustable interest rates that are called floating rate bonds. There is also high yield bonds, which will pay higher coupon rates; however, they have a smaller quality rating. Bonds are able to be purchased as a package in the form of bond exchange traded fund or a bond mutual fund. In retirement bonds can be utilized to form a bond ladder that includes maturity dates. This investment structure is referred to as an asset liability matching or even time segmentation.

5. **Variable Annuity with Lifetime Income Rider**: A variable annuity is different than the type of investment than an immediate annuity. In a variable annuity the money goes into a specified portfolio of investments that you can choose. You will participate in the gains, as well as the losses in these investments; however, for an additional cost you will add guarantees that are called riders. Think of this like a type of umbrella, you may not

need one, but it will protect you if the scenario arises. Riders that offer income will go by different names like living benefit riders, guaranteed benefits for withdraws, lifetime minimum income rider, and more. Each will have a different formula that will determine the type of guarantee being provided.

6. **Keep Safe Investments**: You will want to keep a part of your retirement investments in the safe alternatives. The primary goal of safe investment is to protect yourself rather than generate income. This is to keep things safe for you for the future. In addition, if you are unsure of what you need to do with the money, put it in a safe investment while you take time to ensure you have made an educated decision. There are too many people that rush into investment because they think they should, but it is also risky. It is very important to keep some of the money safe.

7. **Producing Closed End Funds**: The majority of the closed end funds are created to produce a monthly or even quarterly income. This income is able to come from the interest, covered calls, dividends, or from a return of the principal. Each of the fund has its own objective. Some own bonds, others own stocks. There are some that write covered calls in order to generate some income. There are even some that are called dividend capture strategy. You will need to make sure you do research before you purchase them. Some closed end funds utilise leverage, which means that they borrow against securities in the fund in order to purchase more income producing securities.These have a larger payout of income.

8. **Dividend Income Funds**: Instead of purchasing individual stocks that end up paying dividends, you may choose a dividend income fund, which will then own and manage dividend paying stocks. Dividends are able to provide a good and steady source of income for retirement. Many publicly traded businesses and companies produce qualified dividends, which means that they are taxed at a lower rate than an ordinary income or an interest income. For this specific reason, it may be the most tax efficient way to hold funds or some stocks which will produce qualified dividend within accounts that are not for retirement.

9. **Real Estate Investment Trusts**: A real estate investment trust, also called REIT, is much like a mutual fund that owns property. A team of professionals manage this property, pay expenses, collect rent, collect management fees, and will distribute the rest of income to the investor. REITs can specialise in a specific type of property like

apartment building, hotels, motels, or office buildings. There are non-publicly traded real estate investment trusts that can be a good retirement investment. When they are used as a part of a portfolio that is diversified, REITs are a good way to invest for retirement.

## Conclusion

After reading through the investment options you have choices to make. From apartment buildings to stocks and bonds, there are so many ways for you to build up your investment portfolio in order to get your retirement funds to where you would like to have them. Look at what you already have invested in. You may already have a portfolio started and you may not even know it. This is a great start. Now, you can build it further to become rich for retirement.

If you enjoyed this book please be so kind and leave a review if you want to.

Best luck to you!